Animals of Yellowstone

A Children's Book

Bryan Nowak has also authored the following books
that can be purchased at Amazon.com

Photographing Cades Cove
Photographing Roaring Fork Motor Nature Trail
Photographing Smoky Mountain Wildflowers
Photographing the Great Smoky Mountains
MAJESTY

Snowshoe Hare

Table of Contents

Yellowstone's most famous animal is the bison or buffalo.
It stands very tall, has horns and a very strong neck.

Baby buffalo are called calves or red dogs.
They like to jump in the air, play and run very fast.

When a buffalo calf has an itch,
it will scratch on a rock or tree.

Buffalo will march right down the middle of roads.
All traffic comes to a stop for this parade.

Elk look like big deer. This one is shedding his winter coat. The boy elk have antlers that will grow tall and wide.

Baby elk are called fawns.
They have a brown coat of fur with white spots.

Elk fawns are born in the springtime.
They stay very close to their mothers.

Elk live in groups called herds. They rest together in the sage brush and eat in grassy meadows.

Did you know you can see pelicans in Yellowstone?
They don't just live by the ocean.

Pelicans put their mouths (or beaks) in the water as they swim side-by-side together to catch fish.

Pronghorn are the fastest animals in the park.
They run to escape from coyotes, wolves and bears.

Pronghorns get their name from the shape of their antlers. Can you see what looks like hooks on the end?

Black bears are a favorite sight for park visitors. After sleeping all winter, they wake up hungry for something to eat.

Black bears eat a lot of fruits, nuts, insects, honey and fish. This bear is enjoying a nice grass salad.

Bears get sleepy just like you. They make their bed on a log, in a tree, in a hole or anywhere they want.

**This black bear mom is teaching her cubs to
follow the leader — even over big logs.**

**Black bears can also be red or blond in color.
This color is often called "cinnamon."**

Bears are very good swimmers.
They also like to splash and play in the water.

Grizzly bears also make their home in Yellowstone. They have light or dark brown hair and a hump behind their neck.

Just like other little boys and girls, grizzly bear cubs
like to climb on mama's back for a ride.

The bald eagle is a beautiful bird with white feathers on its head and tail. Look in tree tops for eagles.

An eagle has many feathers. These feathers keep the eagle warm but also help it soar in the sky without flapping.

This is a wolf. Some are dark and some are light in color. Wolves live in family groups called packs.

**The coyote looks like a wolf but it is smaller,
with a skinny nose and bushy tail.**

Beavers have wide, flat tails to help them swim.
They live in homes or lodges made of sticks.

Beavers like to eat fresh willow branches using their sharp front teeth. They are shy so be quiet if you want to see a beaver.

Owls live high in trees and can be hard to see.
Their feathers are the same color as the tree.

**Grouse are very good at hiding in the grass.
Can you find this bird?**

Foxes look like dogs or coyotes but their hair is mostly red with white patches. Baby foxes are called kits.

Kits love to run and play with their brothers and sisters. Mother fox must watch them closely.

Mountain goats live high in the mountains.
They have a long, white coat of hair for the snow and cold.

Mountain goats have very good balance.
They can jump and climb on rocks and cliffs.

This is a ram big horn sheep.
I'll bet you can guess where it gets its name.

A baby big horn sheep is called a lamb.
They are very good climbers even as babies.

Marmots live among rocks and boulders.
They look like really big squirrels.

Marmots stand up to look around.
They will run and hide under a rock if they are scared.

**Otters live near Yellowstone's rivers and lakes.
Their favorite food is fish.**

Otters are very good swimmers. They are fun to watch as they play games in the water.

**Moose are large animals and look like a horse.
They live in the woods and visit rivers to eat.**

Moose use their long necks and strong teeth to strip the leaves off branches for food.

A young moose is called a calf. Moose calves eat fresh, green leaves too so they can grow tall like their parents.

**When moose calves get tired they lay down
in the soft grass for a nap.**

The mule deer has very large ears to help it hear better.
It also has a black tip on the end of its tail.

**This is a white-tailed deer. Can you see
the small antlers beginning to grow on its head?**

The osprey flies high in the sky and makes big nests using sticks. It is very good at catching fish in rivers.

Canada geese are found in the park too. Mom and dad are busy with baby goslings born in the spring.

I hope you enjoyed seeing some of the special animals that can be found in Yellowstone National Park.

Which one was your favorite?

I hope one day you too can visit Yellowstone to see many of these same animals for yourself.

Made in the USA
Lexington, KY
23 August 2018